# INTIMACY
## WITH MY
# *Creator*

31 DAY PRAYER DEVOTION

ELIZABETH V. BAEZ

Copyright © Intimacy with My Creator: 31 Day Prayer Devotion
BY
**Elizabeth V. Baez**

Copyright © 2023 by Elizabeth V. Baez

All right reserved. No portion of this book may be reproduced, scanned, stored in a retrieval system, transmitted in any form or by any means- electronically, mechanically, photocopy, recording, or any other- except for brief quotations in printed reviews, without written permission of the publisher. Please do not participate or encourage piracy or copyrighted materials in violation of the author's rights. Purchase only authorized editions.

Bible Translation Copyright ©

KJV Translation-Public Domain

Bible Translation-NIV

THE HOLY BIBLE, NEW INTERNATIONAL VERSION®, NIV® Copyright © 1973, 1978, 1984, 2011 by Biblica, Inc.™ Used by permission. All rights reserved worldwide.

**Bible Translation-ESV**

This publication contains the Holy Bible, English Standard Version®, copyright © 2001 by Crossway Bibles, a publishing ministry of Good News Publishers. ESV Text Edition: 2016. The ESV® text has been reproduced in cooperation with and by permission of Good News Publishers. Unauthorized reproduction of this publication is prohibited. All rights reserved.

Published by Elizabeth V. Baez

Library of Congress Cataloging-in-Publication-Pending

Content Edited by Covered In Dignity Publishing

Book Cover Designed by: Dr. Renee Huffman

Data Publisher and Printing by Elizabeth V. Baez

Written By: Elizabeth V. Baez

Illustrated By: Covered In Dignity Publishing

ISBN: 979-8-218-13041-1

Please contact the author Elizabeth V. Baez @

support@creativeanduniquelearningzone.com

http://www.creativeanduniquelearningzone.com

Please contact Dr. Renee Huffman, Publisher of Covered In Dignity Publishing @ wodmedia@yahoo.com

This Prayer Devotion Belongs to:

_____

# DEDICATION

I dedicate this book to my Lord and Savior Yesuha Hamashiach who gave His life to set me free, to Holy Spirit who comforts me and lead me into all truth, and to the greatest of all Yahweh, I AM, who has thoughts of peace for me and not of evil, desires to give me a great expected end. To my friend, Mrs. Virgie Mae Francois(RIP), a devoted mother, grandmother, great grandmother, great great grandmother. She loved her family and was kind to everyone. I am so grateful she was a part of my life and a wonderful grandmother to my children. She loved the Lord and read devotional books daily. She talked about writing a book someday, but her journey here ended. It is because of her new journey with the Lord in glory, my children are growing even closer to God. My daughter Jovan actually gave me the idea to write a devotional book because of the powerful devotional books she now reads that her grandmother left behind.

# ACKNOWLEDGEMENT

I am extremely grateful to God for calling me out from darkness into His marvelous light.

To my parents, Gail Webb Brumfield and Willis Brumfield for always supporting my dreams. Mother, you often expressed the importance of having a relationship with God and to live a holy and righteous life that would be pleasing to Him I am thankful I had the foundation at an early age you taught me to pray, praise, worship and decree a thing, I appreciate you.

To my children, Gregory (RIP), Jovan, Renee, Shante, Pierre and Jasmine, I am thankful God has given you to me. Each of you have played a role in the person I am today. There were day I felt like giving up or I just could not go on and I pushed and persevered for you my beautiful children.

To my aunt Barbara Red, you always encourage me to relax and breathe and not to work so hard. Do what you can do and don't overdo it, was your message to me. To my aunt Mercedes Nora, you always applauded me and gave me the strength I needed to go on. To my uncle Gerald(RIP) who always told me I can do better and encouraged me never to settle. Thank you all from the bottom of my heart.

To my adorable grandchildren, I am so proud of each one of you. I am grateful for your love and support and always cheering me on. To my smart little old man, my dear great grandson, you do your best to make sure I am on point and doing the right thing. Thank you for your love and tight hugs.

# CONTENTS

**DAY 1:** Sovereign (Supreme Authority) .................................................................. 5

**DAY 2:** Great (Elaborate) ............................................................................................. 8

**DAY 3:** Incredible (Extraordinary) ......................................................................... 11

**DAY 4:** Beautiful (Pleasant) ...................................................................................... 14

**DAY 5:** Strength (Powerful) ...................................................................................... 17

**DAY 6:** Hope (Expect) .................................................................................................. 20

**DAY 7:** Redeemer (Fulfill) .......................................................................................... 23

**DAY 8:** Salvation (Save) .............................................................................................. 26

**DAY 9:** Forgiveness (Pardoned) .............................................................................. 29

**DAY 10:** Freedom (Liberty) ...................................................................................... 32

**DAY 11:** Love (Intimate) ............................................................................................ 35

**DAY 12:** Kindness (Generous) ................................................................................. 38

**DAY 13:** Gentleness (Mildness) ............................................................................... 41

**DAY 14:** Favor (Privilege) ......................................................................................... 44

**DAY 15:** Grace (Courtesy) ......................................................................................... 47

**DAY 16:** Mercy (Compassion) .................................................................................. 50

**DAY 17:** Peace (Tranquil) .......................................................................................... 53

**DAY 18:** Provide (Supply) ......................................................................................... 56

**DAY 19:** Trust (Rely) ................................................................................................... 59

**DAY 20:** Miracle (Divine Manifestation) ............................................................. 62

**DAY 21:** Waymaker (Execute) .................................................................... 65

**DAY 22:** Confident (Believe) ..................................................................... 68

**DAY 23:** Overcomer (Succeed) .................................................................. 71

**DAY 24:** Defeat (Triumphant) .................................................................... 74

**DAY 25:** Gracious (Generous) ................................................................... 77

**DAY 26:** Forsaken (Desert) ....................................................................... 80

**DAY 27:** Believe (Evidence) ...................................................................... 83

**DAY 28:** Exalatation (Praise) ..................................................................... 86

**DAY 29:** Victory (Achieve) ........................................................................ 89

**DAY 30:** Unity (Accord) ............................................................................ 92

**DAY 31:** Rest (Relax) ................................................................................ 95

# MEET THE AUTHOR

Elizabeth V. Baez was born in New Orleans, Louisiana her parents are Willis and Gail Brumfield. She is a loving and supporting mother, dedicated grandmother, and caring great-grandmother. She has devoted her life to God and desires to share the Good News so others may join the Kingdom of God.

Ms. Baez is a servant of God, Yahweh, an advocate, educator, personal life coach, philanthropist, poet, speaker, and bestselling author. She is the founder of Creative and Unique Learning Zone, LLC where she encourages others by sharing life applications and practical principles to live a healthy balanced life by applying the word of God. Founder of Victorious Triumphant Vessel, Inc., where she supports caregivers who provide care for children who are not living with their biological parents, mentors the children and shares love and hope for a bright future.

# INTRODUCTION

It is extremely important to start your day with prayer, praise and worship. We must set aside time to spend with our father. During these private times we will encounter His presence. Prayer and praise will set the tone for our day. The LORD will meet with us to fellowship, lead, guide and instruct us. He will give us wisdom, knowledge, understanding and direction.

God inhabits our praises, and it pleases Him whenever we allow Him to be first in our lives. He gives us free will and never forces us to worship Him. It should be our desire because we love Him. We should never be too busy to spend time with our creator. After all it is because of him that we wake up an experience our day. Without the breath that God breathe on the inside of us we would cease to exist.

I love God with all my heart. I love to pray, praise, and worship. We can pray throughout the day. Prayer is just having a conversation with God. We talked to him, and he responds. Sometimes we ask for things, other times we intercede on the behalf of others, but we should always glorify, magnify, and exalt him daily throughout the day. We are to display gratitude and thankfulness every opportunity we have,for His goodness,

His grace, and His mercy. He is marvelous and magnificent, and he deserves to be praised and reverenced.

This devotional book has many benefits. It will encourage you to memorize scripture, increase your confidence, build your faith and change your prayer life. Please use the reflection page provided for you to meditate on the (daily prayers, scriptures, declarations and decree) to add a written prayer, a scripture that stood out to you to remember and add personalized declarations and decrees. I pray you enjoy your journey.

Prayer Starter

Scriptures from the Holy Bible

Declarations and Decrees

This book was designed to be read at your leisure for daily inspiration for any time of the day. Morning to get your day started, afternoon for an encouraging uplift or for a peaceful covering at the end of your day.

# PRAYER

My God you are *SOVEREIGN*; you are *GREAT*, you are *INCREDIBLE*. Father, you are *BEAUTIFUL* for situations. You are my *STRENGTH*. I have *HOPE* because you are my *REDEEMER*. I thank you for *SALVATION* and for *FORGIVENESS* of my sins. I am extremely grateful for *FREEDOM*, freedom to live, to *LOVE* to show *KINDNESS* for *GENTLENESS*. I give you glory for *FAVOR* on my life. Mere words cannot express my gratitude for your *GRACE* and *MERCY*. I am forever thankful for your *PEACE* that surpasses all understanding. I do not have worry, doubt, or fear because Jireh you are my *PROVIDER*. I *TRUST* in you alone because you have performed extraordinary *MIRACLES* on my behalf and in the lives of others.

I am overjoyed and often overwhelmed because you are my *WAYMAKER* all the time, when there seems to be no way, you make a way. I am CONFIDENT in you because you never have lost a battle. You have *DEFEATED* the enemy time and time again. You are an *OVERCOMER* and so am I. Oh mighty *GRACIOUS* Father you have never abandoned or *FORSAKEN* me; therefore, I have no options except to *BELIEVE in* you. You deserve *EXALTATION* and the highest praise because you have the *VICTORY*. I will walk with my sisters and brothers in *UNITY* and on one accord. I will *REST* in you; and your loving arms will comfort me day and night. I love you Abba Father thank you.

This humble powerful prayer can be prayed daily or weekly. It is a demonstration of gratitude, admiration, praise, and worship to our most High God, also known as JEHOVAH, YAHWEY and the GREAT I AM.

# DAY 1
# SOVEREIGN
(Supreme Authority)

LORD, you are SOVEREIGN, and I bless your holy name. I cry out to you with a loud voice saying Holy, Holy, Holy is the LORD God Almighty, worthy are you LORD. You are High and lifted up and your train fills the temple. All blessing, and honor and glory belong to you alone. You alone are worthy to receive my praise and my worship. I worship you LORD, I worship you with everything in me, I worship you Father.

> **Psalm 46:4**
>
> There is a river whose streams make glad the city of God, the holy habitation of the Most High.

> **Revelation 6:10**
>
> They cried out with a loud voice, "O **Sovereign** Lord, holy and true, how long before you will judge and avenge our blood on those who dwell on the earth?"

> **Acts 4:24**
>
> And when they heard it, they lifted their voices together to God and said, "Sovereign Lord, who made the heaven and the earth and the sea and everything in them,

# DAILY REFLECTION

# Declare and Decree

I know you as a Supreme being a most Holy and righteous God, my Father.

There are no other gods besides you Sovereign God.

My creator is marvelous, and he designed me as an original.

I have everything I need because my God is bigger than everything, He takes great care of me.

I am blessed to have the Sovereign God as my Father

I adore and honor you my King of Kings and LORD of LORD, I am whole.

I love you so much Abba because of your love for me I am secure.

# DAY 2

# GREAT

(ELABORATE)

God you are great and mighty, I am privileged to know you. I am honored to be your child. I am grateful for your love I love you so much oh Great and strong deliver. You are great and greatly to be praised.

> **1 Chronicles 29:11**
>
> Yours, O Lord, is the greatness and the power and the glory and the victory and the majesty, indeed everything that is in the heavens and the earth; Yours is the dominion, O Lord, and You exalt Yourself as head overall.

> **Psalm 96:4**
>
> For great is the Lord and greatly to be praised; He is to be feared above all gods.

> **Acts 4:31**
>
> And when they had prayed, the place in which they were gathered together was shaken, and they were all filled with the Holy Spirit and continued to speak the word of God with boldness.

# DAILY REFLECTION

# Declare and Decree

My God you are so great You cause shaking to take place when I pray.

I will worship you my great and mighty God.

God you are great and greatly to be praised I will praise you no matter what.

Oh great majesty, may I feel your presence throughout this day as I worship you.

My God I expect you do great things for me today.

I will praise your majestic name forevermore for you are great.

I am thankful for your great love for mankind I will tell everyone about you.

# DAY 3
# INCREDIBLE
(EXTRAORDINARY)

Mighty, awesome, Incredible God, I love you so much. You are truly incredible; you have performed so many amazing miracles. You are astonishing and marvelous to me. Every time I think about the way you move the feelings; I experience are indescribable.

> **Revelation 19:6**
>
> Then I heard something like the voice of a great multitude and like the sound of many waters and like the sound of mighty peals of thunder, saying, "Hallelujah! For the Lord our God, the Almighty, reigns.

> **Daniel 3:25**
>
> He answered and said, Lo, I see four men loose, walking in the midst of the fire, and they have no hurt and the form of an the fourth is like the Son of God.

> **Joshua 4:23**
>
> For the LORD your God dried up the waters of Jordan from before you, until ye were passed over, as the LORD your God did to the Red Sea, which he dried up from before us, until we were gone over.

# DAILY REFLECTION

# Declare and Decree

My Father you are incredible, and I will serve you all the days of my life.

LORD, you have and the power to heal me and I receive my healing.

I will rejoice in you my God and you shall allow me to flourish.

I am blessed and highly favored by my incredible God.

All things are working for my good because God is incredible.

You are opening doors for me to walk in and closing door that need to be closed.

You are doing incredible things for all your children.

# DAY 4

# BEAUTIFUL

(Pleasant)

Dear heavenly Father, I believe you sent your son, Jesus to redeem us. Thank you for loving me enough to give your life for me. Thank you for setting me free and giving me victory.

### Psalm 27:4

One thing have I desired of the Lord, that will I seek after; that I may dwell in the house of the Lord all the days of my life, to behold the beauty of the Lord, and to enquire in his temple.

### Psalm 40:5

Many, O Lord my God, are the wonders which You have done, And Your thoughts toward us; There is none to compare with You. If I would declare and speak of them, They would be too numerous to count.

### Isaiah 52:7

How beautiful upon the mountains are the feet of him that bringeth good tidings, that publisheth peace; that bringeth good tidings of good, that publisheth salvation; that saith unto Zion, Thy God reigneth!

# DAILY REFLECTION

# Declare and Decree

The sacrifice Jesus made for me, and all humanity was the greatest love of all.

There is no other God besides my God.

My God is great and mighty.

My God is the first and the last.

My years are being restored.

My life is valuable I have so much to offer the world

I will share the gospel of the Good News

# DAY 5
# STRENGTH
(POWERFUL)

Father I am grateful I can operate in your strength. Your strength is stronger than any other. Thank you for giving me strength, sometimes I feel weak, but I know I am strong. You have strength and power in your mighty hands, and you give strength to me. I receive your strength daily, thank you oh gracious God.

> **Philippians 4:13**
>
> "I can do all things through Christ which strengtheneth me."

> **Psalms 18:1**
>
> I will love thee, O LORD, my strength.

> **Psalm 46:1**
>
> God is our refuge and strength, a very present help in trouble.

> **Exodus 15:2**
>
> The LORD is my strength and song, and he is become my salvation: he is my God, and I will prepare him a habitation; my father's God, and I will exalt him.

# DAILY REFLECTION

# Declare and Decree

My hope is in the Lord my strength is renewed daily.

I am not weak I am strong, for God has strengthened me.

I will declare the strength of my God every day.

I walk in strength because my God gives me strength.

I can do all things through Christ who gives me strength.

I am strong and courageous for the Lord my God is with me everywhere I go.

I am strengthened in the presence of the LORD.

# DAY 6

# HOPE

(EXPECT)

My God, my strong deliver I love you and have hope that you will always be Father and I will always be your child. There is so much for me to live for so many things I must accomplish for your glory. I will not give up I will continue to stand.

> **1 John 3:1**
>
> See what kind of love the Father has given to us, that we should be called children of God; and so, we are. The reason why the world does not know us is that it did not know him.

> **Acts 26:6**
>
> And now I am standing trial for the hope of the promise made by God to our fathers.

> **Romans 15:4**
>
> For whatever was written in earlier times was written for our instruction, so that through perseverance and the encouragement of the Scriptures we might have hope.

# DAILY REFLECTION

# Declare and Decree

I am full of hope I am not hopeless.

I will share the good news with the world so thy will believe and have hope.

My hope is in you my LORD creator of heaven and earth.

Father, I know you think thoughts of peace and a future and a hope for me.

My hope is steadfast because of Jesus Christ's shed blood I have eternal life.

Nothing can shake my faith I will never become hopeless.

I am not tired or weary I am encouraged and full of energy I will stand.

# DAY 7
# REDEEMER
## (FULFILL)

Thank you for redeeming me Lord Jesus for I was lost, and you found me, saved me from damnation and now I can live with you forever. Thank you for being my ransom. I am grateful for the blood you shed for me and my sins. I am redeemed and I am saying so.

> **Nehemiah 1:10**
>
> Now these are thy servants and thy people, whom thou hast redeemed by thy great power, and by thy strong hand.

> **Psalm 130:7**
>
> O Israel, hope in Jehovah; For with Jehovah there is lovingkindness, And with him is plenteous redemption.

> **Exodus 15:13**
>
> Thou in thy lovingkindness hast led the people that thou hast redeemed: Thou hast guided them in thy strength to thy holy habitation.

# DAILY REFLECTION

## Declare and Decree

I am redeemed and I am happy because Jesus redeemed me.

I can always trust in my Redeemer for he has the greatest power.

I am released from captivity because of my Redeemer.

My deliverer has delivered me, all glory be unto God.

I never have to worry about my future it is secured.

My Redeemer is alive and well He is coming back for me one day.

My Redeemer lives and reign and rule forever.

# DAY 8

# SALVATION

(SAVE)

My Jesus thank you for salvation. Only you can save me Yeshua only your blood could sacrifice for me, cleanse me and make me whiter than snow. Oh, lamb of God who takes away the sins of the world I worship you. I live to bless your holy and righteous name. My everlasting Savior and salvation my King of Kings and Lord of Lords. I love you so much.

> **Psalm 18:2**
>
> The LORD is my rock, and my fortress, and my deliverer; my God, my strength, in whom I will trust; my buckler, and the horn of my salvation, and my high tower.

> **Acts 16:31**
>
> And they said, "Believe in the Lord Jesus, and you will be saved, you and your household."

> **Romans 10:9**
>
> Because, if you confess with your mouth that Jesus is Lord and believe in your heart that God raised him from the dead, you will be saved.

> **Psalms 37:39**
>
> The salvation of the righteous is from the Lord; he is their stronghold in the time of trouble.

# DAILY REFLECTION

# Declare and Decree

The truth has sets me free.

I confess with my mouth that you are Lord Yeshua.

I will worship you all the days of my life God of my salvation.

I believe my household and my bloodline will receive salvation.

I am grateful for salvation.

You delivered me and I know I am saved.

# DAY 9
# FORGIVENESS
(Pardoned)

I love you so much Jesus, thank you for forgiving all my sins. I desire to be forgiving as soon as I'm offended. I want to forgive myself. Please continue to help me walk in full forgiveness. May I always know my sins are far from the east is to the west and I do not need to revisit my short comings. I am grateful to you for forgiveness.

**Colossians 3:13**

Bear with each other and forgive one another if any of you has a grievance against someone. Forgive as the Lord forgave you.

**Luke 23:34**

Jesus said, "Father, forgive them, for they do not know what they are doing." And they divided up his clothes by casting lots.

**Ephesians 4:32**

Be kind and compassionate to one another, forgiving each other, just as in Christ God forgave you.

# DAILY REFLECTION

# Declare and Decree

I will walk in forgiveness just as God forgives me, I will forgive others.

I am grateful for the gift to forgive, thank you for forgiving me.

If my brother or sister offend me, I will forgive them.

I will forgive as often, and I am offended.

My sins are forgiven.

I forgive myself and walk in newness.

My sins are as far from the east is to the west.

# DAY 10

# FREEDOM

(LIBERTY)

My Jesus thank you for freedom. Freedom from bondage. No longer am I bound my Lord, my God and for this I give you praise. I glorify your holy name forever. Your mercy and grace endure. Your love is everlasting my King. I am grateful for freedom.

> **Romans 6:22**
>
> But now that you have been set free from sin and have become slaves of God, the fruit you get leads to sanctification and its end, eternal life.

> **2 Corinthians 3:17**
>
> Now the Lord is the Spirit, and where the Spirit of the Lord is, there is freedom.

> **Galatians 5:1**
>
> It is for freedom that Christ has set us free. Stand firm, then, and do not let yourselves be burdened again by a yoke of slavery.

# DAILY REFLECTION

# Declare and Decree

I know the truth and the truth sets me free.

I will worship you all the days of my life LORD.

I walk in freedom and righteousness.

I am a new creature.

I forget the failures and short comings of my past.

I am free from guilt and shame.

I am free to walk according to the spirit.

# DAY 11

# LOVE

(INTIMATE)

Father, your love for me is overwhelming. You loved me so much you sent your son to save me, and I am extremely honored and thankful. It is a privilege to be loved by the Most High God. Abba you are a good father full of love and compassion towards me and I cannot live without your love.

> **Galatians 5:14**
>
> For the entire law is fulfilled in keeping this one command: "Love your neighbor as yourself."

> **Romans 8:35-39**
>
> Who shall separate us from the love of Christ? Shall tribulation, or distress, or persecution, or famine, or nakedness, or peril, or sword?
>
> As it is written, for thy sake we are all the day long; we are accounted as sheep for the slaughter.
>
> Nay, in all these things we are more than conquerors through him that loved us.
>
> For I am persuaded, that neither death, nor life, nor angels, nor principalities, nor powers, nor things present, nor things to come,
>
> Nor height, nor depth, nor any other creature, shall be able to separate us from the love of God, which is in Christ Jesus our Lord.

# DAILY REFLECTION

# Declare and Decree

My Father loves me with an everlasting love.

There is nothing that can come between my father's love and me.

I am filled with love, and I walk in love.

I am thankful to love even the unlovable, I will love my enemies and do good.

I love because Christ first loved me.

God is love; He is the lover of my soul.

I abide in love and abide in God, and God abides in me.

# DAY 12

# KINDNESS

(Generous)

Father it is your desire for me to walk in kindness. I am thankful for your kindness towards humanity. It is a wonderful gift and blessing you have given me. I am pleased to represent you and show kindness toward others. I love you so much and desire to be pleasing to you all the days of my life.

> **1 Corinthians 13:4**
>
> Love is patient, love is kind it does not envy, it does not boast, it is proud.

> **Colossians 3:12**
>
> Therefore, as God's chosen people, holy and dearly loved, clothe yourselves with compassion, kindness, humility, gentleness, and patience.

> **Ephesians 2:6,7**
>
> and raised us up with him and seated us with him in the heavenly places in Christ Jesus,
>
> so that in the coming ages he might show the immeasurable riches of his grace in kindness toward us in Christ Jesus.

# DAILY REFLECTION

## Declare and Decree

It is truly a blessing to walk in kindness, I shall be kind all the days of my life.

Those who I encounter will show me kindness.

I will show kindness to others every day.

Being loving and kind is my portion.

I benefit from being kind.

The teaching of kindness is in my mouth.

As God's chosen vessel I am clothed with kindness.

# DAY 13

# GENTLENESS

(MILDNESS)

Thank you for gentleness oh God. You have giving me the spirit of gentleness. I will exercise a gentle and humble spirit so that you may get the glory from my life. calmness will lay great offenses to rest.

> **1 Timothy 6:11**
>
> But as for you, O man of God, flee these things. Pursue righteousness, godliness, faith, love, steadfastness, gentleness.

> **Titus 3:2**
>
> To speak evil of no one, to avoid quarreling, to be gentle, and to show perfect courtesy toward all people.

> **James 3:17**
>
> But the wisdom from above is first pure, then peaceable, gentle, open to reason, full of mercy and good fruits, impartial and sincere.

# DAILY REFLECTION

# Declare and Decree

I am gentle as a dove.

I possess gentleness.

I express gentleness in my actions and conversations.

I will be gentle like a nursing mother even when others are not being gentle.

I am graced with walking in gentleness daily.

Gentleness is my portion.

# DAY 14

# FAVOR

(PRIVILEGE)

You favor me my God, I am overwhelmed with love when I think about how you have favor for me. There are no words I can use to show how grateful and appreciative I am for the favor you have bestowed upon me. I thank you Father.

> **Luke 2:52**
>
> And Jesus increased in wisdom and in stature and in favor with God and man.

> **Psalm 5:12**
>
> For you bless the righteous, O Lord; you cover him with favor as with a shield.

> **Proverbs 3:3,4**
>
> Let not steadfast love and faithfulness forsake you; bind them around your neck; write them on the tablet of your heart. So, you will find favor and good success in the sight of God and man.

# DAILY REFLECTION

# Declare and Decree

I am favored by God and man.

Unmerited favor knows my name.

I am the apple of my Father's eye.

My father will fulfill all the promises He has for me because of favor.

Favor goes before. Favor follows me. Favor surrounds me.

I have obtained an inheritance, having been predestined according to the purpose of him who works all things according to the counsel of his will.

# DAY 15

# GRACE

(COURTESY)

Your grace is like none other, Abba I am so grateful to you for grace if it had not been for your grace where would I be. The reason I am here is because of your grace and mercy. I love you and I am grateful for your gracious great grace my Savior and Lord.

> **Hebrews 4:16**
>
> Let us then with confidence draw near to the throne of grace, that we may receive mercy and find grace to help in time of need.

> **Ephesians 2:8,9**
>
> For by grace you have been saved through faith. And this is not your own doing; it is the gift of God, not a result of works, so that no one may boast.

> **2 Timothy 2:9**
>
> Who saved us and called us to a holy calling, not because of our works but because of his own purpose and grace, which he gave us in Christ Jesus before the ages began,

> **Titus 2:11**
>
> For the grace of God has appeared, bringing salvation for all people,

# DAILY REFLECTION

# Declare and Decree

Sin has no dominion over me because I am not under the law but under grace.

I am strengthened by the grace that is in Christ Jesus.

I am growing in grace and the knowledge of my Lord.

God has gifted me with grace, and I will use it to serve others.

Grace is my portion.

# DAY 16

# MERCY

(COMPASSION)

When I think about your mercy towards me, I feel so underserving and cannot understand your great love. Your mercy is everlasting, and your truth endures throughout all generations.

> **Proverbs 28:13**
>
> Whoever conceals their sins does not prosper, but the one who confesses and renounces them finds mercy.

> **1 Peter 1:3**
>
> Blessed be the God and Father of our Lord Jesus Christ! According to his great mercy, he has caused us to be born again to a living hope through the resurrection of Jesus Christ from the dead,

> **Daniel 9:9**
>
> The Lord our God is merciful and forgiving, even though we have rebelled against him;

# DAILY REFLECTION

## Declare and Decree

I am blessed to be merciful. My Father is merciful.

I will be merciful to the merciful.

My God has not restrained His mercy from me.

I embrace every day filled with new mercies for me.

God's great mercy caused me to be born again.

My Lord is merciful and gracious, slow to anger and abounding in steadfast love.

The steadfast love of the Lord never ceases; his mercies never come to an end.

# DAY 17

# PEACE

## (TRANQUIL)

I praise you for peace my LORD, peace that only you can give me. Father your peace that passes all understanding, no one can comprehend it. I will keep my mind on you so I can have perfect peace. I need your peace to make it through this journey, sometimes it is hard difficult situations arise, but I know you are for me. Thank you for your wonderful peace.

> **John 16:33**
>
> I have said these things to you, that in me you may have peace. In the world you will have tribulation. But take heart; I have overcome the world.

> **2 Corinthians 13:11**
>
> Finally, brothers, rejoice. Aim for restoration, comfort one another, agree with one another, live in peace; and the God of love and peace will be with you.

> **Philippians 4:9**
>
> What you have learned and received and heard and seen in me—practice these things, and the God of peace will be with you.

# DAILY REFLECTION

# Declare and Decree

I will keep my mind on thee for you give me peace.

The God of peace is with me.

The Lord of peace himself always give me peace in every way.

The peace of Christ Jesus rules in my heart.

I am a peacemaker.

I walk in peace and share the love of God.

My ways are pleasing to the LORD and my enemies are at peace with me.

# DAY 18

# PROVIDE

## (SUPPLY)

Jehovah Jireh you are my provider and I trust you. I know you will meet all my needs according to your riches and glory. I praise you oh great and mighty provider! I am ever so grateful to you for provision. Thank you so much for always providing for me.

> **Psalms 107: 9**
> For he satisfies the longing soul, and the hungry soul he fills with good things.

> **Luke 12:24**
> There Consider the ravens: they neither sow nor reap, they have neither storehouse nor barn, and yet God feeds them. Of much more value are you than the birds!

> **Psalms 4:8**
> In peace I will both lie down and sleep; for you alone. O LORD, make me dwell in safety.

> **Galatians 5:22,**
> But the fruit of the Spirit is love, joy, peace, patience, kindness, goodness, faithfulness,

# DAILY REFLECTION

## Declare and Decree

I am healed and whole, God provides me with strength and health.

The LORD provides me with wisdom, knowledge and understanding.

God satisfies my soul.

God provides spiritual and physical food for me.

My God gives me peaceful rest and keep me safe from harm.

I have joy, peace, and love provided from my Father.

# DAY 19

# TRUST

(RELY)

Jesus you trusted God to be with you during your journey in this earth and I thank you for deciding to come and save humanity. You did not trust in man, and I chose to follow your example by only trusting our Father. I trust you God for being faithful to us all. Thank you for not abandoning or forsaking us.

**Psalm 119:8**

It is better to trust in the LORD than to put confidence in man.

**Isaiah 12:2**

Behold, God is my salvation; I will trust, and not be afraid: for the LORD JEHOVAH is my strength and my song; he also is become my salvation.

**Isaiah 26:3**

You keep him in perfect peace whose mind is stayed on you, because he trusts in you.

# DAILY REFLECTION

# Declare and Decree

I am trusting God alone for He will never fail me.

I will walk in righteousness and will flourish like a green leaf.

I trust God to always come through for me.

I do not put my trust in any other source besides my God.

I trust God will all my heart and do not lean to my own understanding.

The Lord is my strength and my shield; in him my heart trusts.

I will not trust in richest.

I will walk in righteousness and will flourish like a green leaf.

# DAY 20

# MIRACLE

(Divine Manifestation)

Father you are a great and awesome miracle worker. You perform miraculously and marvelously with beauty and wonder. I am in awe of you and thankful to you for all the

miracles you have performed in my life and the lives of others. I stand in amazement of your miraculous power it is extraordinary, there is none besides you who can perform miracles like you.

**Matthew 9:27-30**

And as Jesus passed on from there, two blind men followed him, crying aloud, "Have mercy on us, Son of David." When he entered the house, the blind men came to him, and Jesus said to them, "Do you believe that I am able to do this?" They said to him, "Yes, Lord." Then he touched their eyes, saying, "According to your faith be it done to you." And their eyes were opened. And Jesus sternly warned them, "See that no one knows about it.

**Acts 2:22**

"Men of Israel, hear these words: Jesus of Nazareth, a man attested to you by God with mighty works and wonders and signs that God did through him in your midst, as you yourselves know—

# DAILY REFLECTION

## Declare and Decree

Miracles signs and wonders will follow those who believe.

I believe in the miraculous acts that Jesus performed, and I believe miracles are still being performed today.

I have the power working on the inside of me to touch others and God will miraculously heal them.

I can do all things through Christ who gives me strength.

There is nothing impossible with God.

# DAY 21

# WAYMAKER

(EXECUTE)

Waymaker that is who you are. You have made ways when there seemed to be no way. You open doors that no man can open and you shut doors no man can shut. Thank you for always making a way for me. I can always count on you to make a way.

> **Isaiah 43:15-21**
>
> I am the Lord, your Holy One, the Creator of Israel, your King." Thus says the Lord, who makes a way in the sea, a path in the mighty waters, who brings forth chariot and horse, army and warrior; they lie down, they cannot rise, they are extinguished, quenched like a wick: "Remember not the former things, nor consider the things of old. Behold, I am doing a new thing; now it springs forth, do you not perceive it? I will make a way in the wilderness and rivers in the desert.

> **John 2:22,23**
>
> When therefore he was raised from the dead, his disciples remembered that he had said this, and they believed the Scripture and the word that Jesus had spoken. Now when he was in Jerusalem at the Passover Feast, many believed in his name when they saw the signs that he was doing.

# DAILY REFLECTION

# Declare and Decree

God is always making a way for me.

I never have to worry or doubt God is working it out for my good.

The Lord never sleeps nor slumber He watches over me both night and day.

He will do exactly what He says He will do.

There is nothing too hard for God for He is the LORD God of all flesh.

I humble myself under the mighty hand of God.

# DAY 22
# CONFIDENT
(BELIEVE)

Majestic, omnipotent, omnipresent, wonderful God I am confident that you will fight my battles. You have created all things with just speaking it into existing, how much more can you help me. You are my defender and protector. You have given me so many things to enjoy while living in this world. I am grateful to you for it all.

> **Genesis 1:1-5**
> In the beginning, God created the heavens and the earth. The earth was without form and void, and darkness was over the face of the deep. And the Spirit of God was hovering over the face of the waters. And God said, "Let there be light," and there was light. And God saw that the light was good. And God separated the light from the darkness. God called the light Day, and the darkness he called Night. And there was evening and there was morning, the first day.

> **Acts 2:1-5**
> When the day of Pentecost arrived, they were all together in one place. And suddenly there came from heaven a sound like a mighty rushing wind, and it filled the entire house where they were sitting. And divided tongues as of fire appeared to them and rested on each one of them. And they were all filled with the Holy Spirit and began to speak in other tongues as the Spirit gave them utterance. Now there were dwelling in Jerusalem Jews, devout men from every nation under heaven.

# DAILY REFLECTION

# Declare and Decree

Whatever I ask in prayer I have confidence I will receive it because I am in my Father's will.

God gave me confidence to win in every circumstance and situation.

I give God glory for confidence not in myself but in Him

The Lord is my confidence.

I am confident that God sees, hears and is with me.

I do not have to fear I have confidence in my God.

Confidence is my portion.

I live a confident lifestyle because I am a child of God.

# DAY 23
# OVERCOMER
## (Succeed)

It is because you are an overcomer so am I. You overcame and defeated death and I am overcoming by the blood of the lamb and the words of my testimony. Thank you for being the greatest overcomer. I will glorify you and worship you forever and ever.

> **John 16:33**
>
> I have said these things to you, that in me you may have peace. In the world you will have tribulation. But take heart; I have overcome the world."

> **1 John 3:3-5**
>
> For this is the love of God, that we keep his commandments. And his commandments are not burdensome. For everyone who has been born of God overcomes the world. And this is the victory that has overcome the world—our faith. Who is it that overcomes the world except the one who believes that Jesus is the Son of God?

> **Numbers 13:30**
>
> But Caleb quieted the people before Moses and said, "Let us go up at once and occupy it, for we are well able to overcome it."

# DAILY REFLECTION

# Declare and Decree

You reign forever and ever and are seated in heavenly places, I shall overcome.

I will conquer and God will grant me to eat of the tree of life, which is in paradise.

I am not conformed to this world; I am transformed by the renewing of my mind.

God overcame the world, and he abides in me.

Greater is He that is inside of me than he that is in the world.

# DAY 24

# DEFEAT

(Triumphant)

You conquered and defeated death, there's no one greater. You are victorious, magnificent, and triumphant. I love how you show up for me, rescuing my soul, saving me from trouble. You are undefeated and I am happy that you are my God. You come in an instance to help me, I walk in blessings because you defeat the enemy who tries to curse me. Father, you have defeated lack and poverty in my life and I will forever glorify your holy and righteous name, Abba.

Missing the Scripture Romans 6:1-2.

> **1 Peter 5:7-9**
>
> Casting all your anxieties on him because he cares for you. Be sober-minded; be watchful. Your adversary the devil prowls around like a roaring lion, seeking someone to devour. Resist him, firm in your faith, knowing that the same kinds of suffering are being experienced by your brotherhood throughout the world.

There is therefore now no condemnation for those who are in Christ Jesus

For the law of the Spirit of life has set you free in Christ Jesus from the law of sin and death.

# DAILY REFLECTION

## Declare and Decree

I am not defeated. I am victorious.

I only listen to the voice of the Most High God.

Because of the blood Jesus I am not defeated

By Jesus stripes I am healed, delivered and undefeated.

I sit in heavenly places with my King.

I bind my mind to the mind of Christ and that mind is not a defeated mindset.

# DAY 25

# GRACIOUS

(Generous)

Oh, holy gracious God you are omnipotent and wonderful. My heart sing praises to you and great are you, my Lord. There is none that compares to you. Nobody like you in all the earth and above the earth in the heavens you are so amazing to me. I marvel at your graciousness. I love you Abba.

> **Genesis 2:7**
>
> Then the Lord God formed the man of dust from the ground and breathed into his nostrils the breath of life, and the man became a living creature.

> **Acts 17:25**
>
> Nor is he served by human hands, as though he needed anything, since he himself gives to all mankind life and breath and everything.

> **Psalm 103:8-12**
>
> The Lord is merciful and gracious, slow to anger and abounding in steadfast love. He will not always chide, nor will he keep his anger forever. He does not deal with us according to our sins, nor repay us according to our iniquities. For as high as the heavens are above the earth, so great is his steadfast love toward those who fear him; as far as the east is from the west, so far does he remove our transgressions from us.

# DAILY REFLECTION

# Declare and Decree

The gracious hand of my God is upon me.

I am a gracious child of God.

My God's grace is sufficient for me.

By my Father's power I am made perfect in weakness.

My gracious Father makes me strong when I am weak.

The Spirit of God has made me, and the breath of the Almighty gives me life.

God's breath blows on me daily, I am graciously covered.

# DAY 26

# FORSAKEN

(Desert)

Father, God you have never forsaken me and never will, I am grateful. You are faithful and slow to anger I know you will not abandon or forsake me. I will remain in position in a posture of prayer and thanksgiving because you love me so much. I will not forsake you my sweet Savior. I will not turn away from you, my strong and mighty God.

> **Psalm 37:27-29**
>
> Turn away from evil and do good; so shall you dwell forever. For the Lord loves justice; he will not forsake his saints. They are preserved forever, but the children of the wicked shall be cut off. The righteous shall inherit the land and dwell upon it forever.
>
> **Ezekiel 18:4**
>
> Behold, all souls are mine; the soul of the father as well as the soul of the son is mine: the soul who sins shall die.
>
> **Titus 1:2**
>
> In hope of eternal life, which God, who never lies, promised before the ages began

# DAILY REFLECTION

# Declare and Decree

I am not forsaken I am not forgotten I am loved by God.

God desires for me to be saved and to come to the knowledge of the truth.

I have never seen the righteous or forsaken their children begging bread and I never will.

I am grateful God has never forsaken me.

I will never forsake my God, because I honor Him and love Him. I am confident God will never forsake me nor will He ever leave me.

# DAY 27

# BELIEVE

(EVIDENCE)

My mighty King of Kings and Lord of Lords the great I am, I love you so much. I am forever grateful to you Jesus for the loving gift of eternal life. I believe you gave your life for me. I believe you rose from the dead and when you got up you rose with all power.

> **John 7:38**
>
> He that believeth on me, as the scripture hath said, out of his belly shall flow rivers of living water.

> **1 Timothy 4:10**
>
> For therefore we both labor and suffer reproach, because we trust in the living God, who is the Savior of all men, specially of those that believe.

> **Hebrews 11:6**
>
> But without faith it is impossible to please him: for he that cometh to God must believe that he is, and that he is a rewarder of them that diligently seek him.

# DAILY REFLECTION

# Declare and Decree

I believe out of my belly will flow rivers of living water.

I will trust in the Sovereign God forever no matter what it looks like in the natural.

I walk by faith and not by sight.

I am pleasing to God.

I diligently seek my Father.

God rewards me daily.

I rejoice with unspeakable joy and full of glory.

# DAY 28

# EXALATATION

(Praise)

I exalt thee oh Mighty King. You are great and greatly to be praised I worship you in spirit and truth. I adore and honor you my master, my Lord my everything. I magnify you and lift you up high. Above the heavens is your dwelling place yet you abide within me. I glorify you alone my abba father I love you so much.

> **Psalm 46:10**
>
> "Be still and know that I am God. I will be exalted among the nations; I will be exalted in the earth!"

> **Isaiah 25:1**
>
> O Lord, you are my God; I will exalt you; I will praise your name, for you have done wonderful things, plans formed of old, faithful, and sure.

> **Psalm 99:5**
>
> Exalt the Lord our God; worship at his footstool! Holy is he!

# DAILY REFLECTION

# Declare and Decree

I am a holy nation, a royal priesthood

I will exalt you giver of life, you have great hopes for me.

I exalt your word for it is living and active and sharper than any two-edged sword.

I exalt thy excellency for you have called me out of darkness into your marvelous light.

I will sing to the Lord, for he is highly exalted.

"I will praise my Rock and my Savior for He is worthy, and He is exalted.

# DAY 29

# VICTORY

(ACHIEVE)

Father, God, thank you for victory I am so happy I am victorious because of you. There is power in the name of Jesus to save and to loosen chains and to set free. I live an abundantly victorious because of you. I love you and am ever so grateful for victory over the enemy.

> **Deuteronomy 20:1-4**
>
> "When you go out to war against your enemies and see horses and chariots and an army larger than your own, you shall not be afraid of them, for the Lord your God is with you, who brought you up out of the land of Egypt. And when you draw near to the battle, the priest shall come forward and speak to the people and shall say to them, 'Hear, O Israel, today you are drawing near for battle against your enemies: let not your heart faint. Do not fear or panic or be in dread of them, for the Lord your God is he who goes with you to fight for you against your enemies, to give you the victory.'

> **Revelation 21:6.7**
>
> And he said to me, "It is done! I am the Alpha and the Omega, the beginning and the end. To the thirsty I will give from the spring of the water of life without payment. The one who conquers will have this heritage, and I will be his God and he will be my son.

# DAILY REFLECTION

# Declare and Decree

I walk in Victory. I live a victorious lifestyle.

Victory is mine I am victorious.

I am victorious because the LORD loves me

I receive victory because I remain steadfast under trials.

God makes a way of escape for me; therefore, I remain victorious in every situation.

The LORD goes with me to fight for me against my enemies and gives me victory.

With God I gain the victory to trample over the enemy.

# DAY 30

# UNITY

(ACCORD)

Father, I praise you for unity. I thank you for allowing me to walk united with my brothers and sisters in Christ. I glorify you that we are on one accord! Please continue to order my steps and show me the things I need to do to stay aligned with you. I desire to do all that you require of me to be on one accord with you Father.

> **1 Peter 3:8,9**
> Finally, all of you, have unity of mind, sympathy, brotherly love, a tender heart, and a humble mind. Do not repay evil for evil or reviling for reviling, but on the contrary, bless, for to this you were called, that you may obtain a blessing.

> **2 Corinthians 13:11**
> Finally, brothers, rejoice. Aim for restoration, comfort one another, agree with one another, live in peace; and the God of love and peace will be with you.

> **Ephesians 4 :1-6**
> I therefore, a prisoner for the Lord, urge you to walk in a manner worthy of the calling to which you have been called, with all humility and gentleness, with patience, bearing with one another in love, eager to maintain the unity of the Spirit in the bond of peace. There is one body and one Spirit-as you were called to the one hope that belongs to your call-one Lord, one faith, one baptism,

# DAILY REFLECTION

# Declare and Decree

I walk in unity daily with my loved ones.

My joy is complete by being in full accord and of one mind with other believers.

I will take no part in unfruitful works of darkness, but instead expose them.

My God of endurance and encouragement has granted me to live in harmony.

There will be no divisions among my sisters and brothers.

My fellow believers and I are united in the same mind and the same judgment.

# DAY 31

# REST

(Relax)

I am safe and secured in your arms Father, I can rest and have peace with you. I love to rest in your presence, you give me a sweet rest you ease my troubled mind. Thank you for being the greatest one, the magnificent one, the one who gives me rest. When there is so much going on around me I can run to you and you always soothe me and make me feel better. I love you so much Abba.

> **Ecclesiastes 10:4**
>
> If the anger of the ruler rises against you, do not leave your place, for calmness will lay great offenses to rest.

> **John 14:27**
>
> Peace, I leave with you; my peace I give to you. Not as the world gives do I give to you. Let not your hearts be troubled, neither let them be afraid.

> **Matthew 11:28-30**
>
> Come to me, all you who are weary and burdened, and I will give you rest. Take my yoke upon you and learn from me, for I am gentle and humble in heart, and you will find rest for your souls. For my yoke is easy and my burden is light."

# DAILY REFLECTION

## Declare and Decree

I will rest in the LORD.

I am resting on the assurance my father is for me.

I do not have to get weary in well doing I can rest and remain faithful.

Rest is my portion.

My Lord has given me rest from pain and turmoil.

# Combination of Thirty-One Songs

You are the **Sovereign** God bigger than all my problems, and I praise you by singing How **Great** is our God, sing with me for He is an Incredible God and **Incredible** God deserves an Incredible praise. What a **Beautiful** name it is, the name of Jesus Christ my King, you are my **Strength**, strength like no other. My **Hope** is built on nothing less than Jesus blood and righteousness. My **Redeemer** lives I know my redeemer lives, hallelujah, **Salvation,** and glory and honor and power unto the LORD our God.

Help me now to do the impossible, **Forgiveness** in your name oh God. Where the spirit of the Lord is there is **Freedom.** Your **Love** never fails never runs out, you loving **Kindness** is better than life. Pass me not oh **Gentle** Savior because I'm walking in the **Favor** of God and Your **Grace** and **Mercy** has brought me through. You are the prince of **Peace** God **Provides** in ways I can't explain and can't deny I have no choice but to **Trust** in God and never doubt. He is a M*iracle* worker, promise keeper **Way maker.** I can face my giants with **Confidence,** and so can you because Your **Overcomer** stay in the fight till the final round if your heart under fire, facing **Defeat** close to surrender do not give up. **Gracious** God mighty one on high I thank you I have never seen the righteous **Forsaken**

No matter what the situation I **Believe** I believe no matter what the circumstances I believe I stand on your word I stand on your promise, I **Exalt** thee I have **Victory** in Jesus my Savior forever. We stand together and sing in **Unity.** So I'll **Rest** right here with you.

# DAILY REFLECTION

# DAILY REFLECTION

# DAILY REFLECTION

# DAILY REFLECTION

# DAILY REFLECTION

# DAILY REFLECTION

# DAILY REFLECTION

# DAILY REFLECTION

# DAILY REFLECTION

# DAILY REFLECTION

# DAILY REFLECTION

# DAILY REFLECTION

# DAILY REFLECTION

# DAILY REFLECTION

# DAILY REFLECTION

# DAILY REFLECTION

# DAILY REFLECTION

# DAILY REFLECTION

# DAILY REFLECTION

# DAILY REFLECTION

Made in the USA
Columbia, SC
05 June 2025